Wild Intuition:

An Adventure in Creative Awareness

Melissa Wild

Wild Intuition: An Adventure in Creative Awareness

Melissa Wild

Copyright © 2022 Melissa Wild

Melissa Wild is available to speak at your business or conference event on a variety of topics. Call (585) 813-5548 or email melissawildinsight@gmail.com for booking information.

Table of Contents:

Chapter 1:

Introduction

Imagine spending twenty years ignoring your intuition.

A recurrent nightmare haunted me for months. I dreamt night after night that my mother would die soon. At the time, I was a teenager horrified by a feeling of impending doom. I had an inner sense of knowing that this recurrent nightmare was a warning of imminent loss. The nightmare recurred until the night of my father's sudden and unexpected death.

I rejected the fact that I knew something terrible would happen before it happened. I never wanted to experience this gut-wrenching, tragic inner sense of knowing ever again. I did everything I could think of to disconnect from my intuition. I shut down.

For the next twenty years, I rejected any hint of intuition, whether it was a dream, an emotion, a gut feeling, or any other warning sign. I ignored every clue, whether it was subtle or a boldly obvious warning of disaster to follow. Ignoring my intuition caused many difficult years full of struggle. As the years went by, decision-making became treacherously painful. Every decision I made was the wrong decision. Adversity summarizes twenty years of my life.

A new way of life needed to start emerging. I wanted to transform my life. A fifteen-minute excursion changed my entire approach to life.

As graduate students at Buffalo State University Center for Applied Imagination, we were instructed to spend fifteen minutes outside observing. While outside walking around the campus, it was as if I were experiencing the world for the first time—as if I had never been there before. I was aware of things I hadn't noticed before: so many connections were revealed.

I took notes of my observations of the bark on the trees and the people walking on campus. I discovered how the bark on a tree had grown entirely over where a branch had been removed. The new growth created a beautiful design. It was a sign of regeneration and resilience. I noticed a woman on campus walk to a red convertible. She was wearing red cowboy boots and a red leather jacket. I wrote the thoughts as they entered my mind. *Be bold. Be brilliant. Authenticity is beautiful and radiant.*

Adventure

From this point forward, life became an adventure in creative awareness. I could find new meaning in the world around me and in the pictures I would take. I could connect everything and anything back to the questions in my mind. Answers were everywhere. I became more open to introspective ways of knowing and trusting my wild.

Creative awareness became an adventure that awakened my wild intuition. I realized that intuition, coupled with the intellectual ability to make meaningful connections, leads the way to a life of creative awareness. I found ways to connect my love of nature—taking pictures, writing, and listening to music—to connect with my intuition. I was always eager to learn more. The more knowledge you have, the more prepared you will be for any situation. This is the point where intellect and intuition unite.

Finding meaning within and from external resources was the foundation of defining creative awareness and developing methods to awaken and enhance wild intuition. From here, I began to share this exciting way of seeing the world with others so that they could discover their wild.

By pursuing your curiosity and going on an adventure, this book will teach you how to develop your creative consciousness and become more in tune with your intuition. By developing your creative awareness, you will strengthen your ability to trust your intuition and know that you are following the best path available to you at the moment. As you proceed with the activities in this book, you will feel inspired to explore the world around you. You will find meaningful connections everywhere as you venture on a journey of discovery within yourself and in the world surrounding you. Sometimes the intuitive message is right in front of you, and other times it is found within you. Your intuition is there to guide you. You have all that you need within you to make beautiful moments infinite. Would you like guidance to access your intuition easily?

Adventure exists in the beautiful moments of connection with your surroundings and intuition. This book will take you on an adventure in creative awareness in which you will follow your curiosity and connect with your wild intuition. If you are open and follow your curiosity, you will enhance your intuition and discover the beauty and meaningful connections around you. Wherever you are and wherever you go, adventure will find you.

Stories will describe the presentation of intuition in day-to-day life. The activities will show you how to recognize the subtle signs of intuition and help you discover what they mean to you. You will access resourceful internal states through introspective techniques. Action steps will guide you in applying each technique. The methods are transformative and dynamic with each unique individual's application.

Creative awareness will enhance the way you experience the world. It will inspire you to look at the world around you from different perspectives to find things you didn't know were right there all along. As you travel, you'll learn there is more to see. You will find beauty and magic in everyday life. You will make connections with nature and signs and songs. Creative awareness is led by curiosity and wonder that will take you to your wild.

Wild Intuition

Wild is an authentic natural untamed way of life. Your wild is the combination of your inner voice, thoughts, feelings, dreams, and desires. Wild naturally occurs within every individual. Wild represents your unique individuality. Your wild is like your fingerprint, identifying you as your truest self. Wild is developed through interactions with the environment around us and knowledge from life experiences. Only you can discover and know your wild. As you allow your wild to surface, you will strengthen access to your intuition. You will increase your intuition by engaging with your wild, uncharted energetic navigation and allowing it to lead.

Intuition is like research that will lead you on an adventure. The more you seek, the more you will find. You may follow a butterfly to a flower or a book to an author, which leads to another book. When you stay opportunistic, you will discover transformational expressions of intuition in beautiful ways you never knew existed.

Wild has the potential to become a way of life. What began as something saved for a special occasion, when I would let the wild out and be my unrestrained authentic self, has evolved into my way of life. I suppressed my wild for the longest time, which shut down my intuition. Over time I slowly applied my wild style to my life.

It took twenty years, but I have fully embodied my wild. I even legally changed my last name to Wild. I will share stories from the depth to the altitude and magnitude of my wild. In the action steps, you will discover your particular style of wild, how your wild shows up in your life, and how to connect it to the wisdom within. You will awaken your wild intuition.

Wild intuition made my scuba dream come true. I was swimming fast, fighting against the kelp, the surf, the surge, and the current as I followed the group of divers I had been paired with on the dive briefing. Then I got an intense leg cramp. I did not want to continue. I was disappointed. I could miss the chance to scuba dive with sea lions in the Channel Islands' kelp forest off the coast of California. At one of the safety stops on the way to the surface, I accidentally overinflated my buoyancy control device. I dangerously went to the surface way too fast. Fortunately, I was only in fifteen to eighteen feet of water at this stop. All signs indicated that enough was enough. The dive was over. It had to be. I chose to end the dive rather than continue to struggle and potentially create a dangerous medical condition known as decompression sickness or the bends.

I crawled across the thick kelp forest and swam to the boat. The cramp subsided. The crew suggested ditching the gear and snorkeling for the remainder of the dive. It sounded great to me as it wouldn't be a total loss, and I could stay in the water. I eagerly removed the heavy gear and got back into the ocean. I had no idea that I would soon have the most incredible dive experience of my life.

As I floated along the surface, sea lions approached and surrounded me. The sea lions swam around me, diving below and surfacing next to me. This was beyond what I ever would have imagined. It was as though I had joined the rookery. I spent the next two dives and the remainder of the day floating among the sea lions. It was a peaceful and majestic feeling of pure joy and amazement at all that exists in the wild ocean.

I felt freedom without the heavy gear or the pressure to keep up with the group. The freedom to do my own thing and be among the sea lions was phenomenal. As a result of listening to my intuition, I naturally interacted with the sea lions—an experience I will always cherish. I realized that going deep is not always necessary. Sometimes all the beauty and the essence are at the surface level. I learned to enjoy whatever level presents itself and have carried this quality into other aspects of my life.

Intuition is a solo journey within. The more you put into the adventure, the more you will get out of it. As you are the guide of your adventure, you will find whatever you seek. Each individual finds meaning in the things around them based on their life experiences and view of the world. You will discover validity in applying the techniques as you find meaning in the most unexpected places. You have the freedom to use the activities in the way that best resonates with you.

Messages appear in different ways for different people. Everyone has unique attributes and varied backgrounds that impact their perceptions and interactions. Each of us has our own internal library of resources consisting of knowledge, life experiences, abilities, and instincts. As we interact with the world, we also build our own library of knowledge within. Your own library is an evolutionary process that will continue to grow throughout your life. The surrounding environment shapes us. The available information resources influence intuitive messages. We accept what is true for us at the time. We go with the information and resources we have at the time. A message may appear at any given moment. Messages will appear in ways you will notice, and the more alert and receptive you are, the more frequent and plentiful the messages will become. Appreciation for minor signs leads to attentiveness to more significant signs. Recognizing signs begins the path of wild intuition.

Chapter Intentions

This introductory chapter shared the foundation of the concept. The following provides a description of the chapters ahead to prepare you for the journey.

Chapter 2 will help you to navigate beyond the blocks in the way of intuition.

Chapter 3 teaches the concept of creative awareness and builds excitement for the adventure.

Chapter 4 begins the journey by awakening the senses and reframing disruptive emotional states.

Chapter 5 establishes a geographic connection.

Chapter 6 develops observational skills while appreciating nature.

Chapter 7 asks questions and finds the answers from within and from the environment.

Chapter 8 imagines as if and captures the moments of changing perspectives with a camera.

Chapter 9 follows the lyrics to access musical intuition.

Chapter 10 discusses and instructs on intuitive writing techniques.

Chapter 11 reveals that intuition occurs whether awake or asleep and interprets the messages that appear in dreams and nightmares.

Chapter 12 intends to inspire you, the reader, to continue the journey and live your wild.

Chapter 2:

Navigation

Dreams

The end is seen at the beginning and ends as it begins. If you are receptive, you may visit the future as you start. What if we listened to our intuition right from the start?

As I prepared to move to Florida, I dreamt that my lawyer was a road flagger waving traffic through. Oddly, I was on an amusement park roller coaster ride coming down the hill approaching my New York home. As soon as I woke up, I wrote the dream's message. "The end is seen at the beginning and ends as it begins. Eyes wide open to see. Ask questions. No guessing. Don't let any chance of things not going according to plan keep me from going."

Finding pet-friendly housing across the country was a challenge. Only one apartment allowed two Jack

Russell terriers, a cat, and a pigeon. On the map, the place seemed too far inland to satisfy my desire to live the beach life. I ignored this detail.

Upon our arrival in Florida, my son and I drove to the apartment's location. The busyness of the area and the far distance from the beach were unappealing. We both got a bad vibe that we could not explain from the complex itself. The bad vibes were ignored.

One night long before any plan to move, I made a request. "Dreams, please share with me what my next steps are."

That night I dreamt I was violated, exploited, and had no privacy as if I were living in a dorm room. I felt repulsed and trapped as if people were trying to take advantage of me. Something about this seemed familiar, like it was the same nightmare I kept having presented in a new format. In addition, I was aware that I was dreaming. Within the dream, I heard my voice say, "Never walk out on your dreams. Move forward along the path and stay the course."

The dream concluded with the following action steps: "Live my life and make choices to improve my life."

While living in Florida, the songs entering my mind grew increasingly dark, foreshadowing the need for change. "The Worst Day Ever" by Simple Plan[1] and "Sabotage" by the Beastie Boys[2] played in my mind. It was a playlist that needed to change. There was also a persistent song of hope, indicating that life would improve. "This Too Shall Pass" by OK Go[3] was constantly on every radio station I chose at that time. It was a song that I could not ignore.

Disaster struck at the apartment complex three months after moving in. In retrospect, I could look at all the intuitive warnings and say we should never have moved into that apartment. Reality paralleled the dream when the apartment felt like a dorm room with people in and out constantly. I felt like I had no privacy. In the end, I followed the action steps in the dream and made choices to improve my life. We returned to where we started. We moved back to our original home in New York. The clear, intuitive return felt accelerated in both speed and ease of transition. Just like the dream, it ended as it began.

Messages

On the drive from Florida back to New York, signs showed we were on the best path forward. There was a

---

[1] Simple Plan. (2002). "The Worst Day Ever." *No Pads, No Helmets...Just Balls*. Lava Records. Atlantic Records.

[2] Beastie Boys. (1994). "Sabotage." *Ill Communication*. Grand Royal Records. Capitol Records.

[3] OK Go. (2010). "This Too Shall Pass." *Of the Blue Colour of the Sky*. Capitol Records.

sign on a truck about the Great Lakes and a road sign for Prosperity Road. The signs triggered intuitive messages. "There will be a fresh perspective on the inland sea." "Become more distinguished and evolve." "Stay inspired and take an alternate route to prosperity."

Intuition serves as a guidepost along the way. It's meant to lead us onto the best path forward. When we ignore our intuition, we choose to put ourselves on the worst trajectory, even though we are unlikely to realize the full magnitude at the time. Sometimes we are so set on achieving a particular outcome that we miss the signs indicating that the way we choose will not work.

There are many circumstances in which we may oppose listening to our intuition. There may be times when you push back against your intuition. Do you ever look back and think, *I knew that would happen? If only I had followed my instincts.*

Let's consider some things that may have stopped you from following your inner guidance.

Perhaps you were impatient and rushing to do what you wanted, like I was on the move to Florida. You may wish to control what happens, or you are determined to achieve a particular outcome no matter what. Intuition arrives in various ways. One sign could have been enough of an indication, and when ignored, many signs collaboratively reveal the same thing. For me, the dreams, the songs, and the bad vibes were all telling me the same thing.

Do you look for the signs you hope to find while ignoring the obvious? Do you seek to verify every detail with research before trusting what you already know? What if you trusted what you intuitively already knew? What if you allowed your intuition to guide you? You can make better-informed choices if you trust that your intuition shows you the best path forward.

Consider for a moment that you focus on the objective truth of the observation and document what you notice with absolute truth. For just a moment, acknowledge and imagine the value of the message in its given form. This will allow you to distinguish the truth beyond projection. Living in truth allows freedom to be.

Write everything that comes to mind while you are in the moment. Even when you try to project the message you desire, the truth will be documented in your objective observation. The intuitive message will be revealed when you read it later, and you are no longer connected to the message you hope to project.

This is a small sample of the action steps you will encounter in the chapters ahead meant to help you express what is there to be revealed.

Sometimes personal preferences conflict with your strongest inner guidance. Rigid adherence to routines and personal preferences may cause mental resistance that keeps you trapped. To go beyond, release the preferences that create the shell boundary of limitation. Release them to clear the way forward. Venture beyond preferences and expectations to overcome stagnation by allowing intuitive discovery. When you are receptive to your strongest intuitive senses, you can apply them to navigate the way forward. Dreams and music are among my strongest intuitive senses, and I have learned to trust them as a guide along the way. As you apply your strongest senses for navigation, the clarity makes the way appear more readily.

Do you ever experience uncertainty about your chosen direction? Have you considered why you are doing something? Perhaps because someone convinced you that it's what you want? Conformity presents another obstruction: it holds us back when we stay in line. We follow the crowd and remain stuck on the illusory path to success. Are there times when you listen to the opinions of others and silence your own voice? Have you struggled to make something work? Imagine that no matter what you try, it does not work. A definitive no is not necessarily rejection; it's simply unavailability, a blocked path guiding you to find another route. When you are aware of limitations, you can move beyond them. If the way is blocked, consider looking toward what naturally works for you. Your wild is what comes naturally. What is your wild? Allow your intuition to show the way to your natural destination.

Perhaps you are afraid of intuitive messages. Are you afraid of receiving a dark message? Your intuition protects you. If a dark message arrives, know that it is just a protective guidepost of a direction to change. It is as an indication that there is something even better awaiting that your wild intuition will guide you to. Move in the direction of your wild and keep momentum.

Be Open

The unfamiliar may appear uniquely strange. Sometimes the intellect analyzes the intuition's subtle and silly presentation, dismissing it as irrelevant. Other times it is difficult to understand and decipher the cryptic code of intuition. As the unfamiliar course appears, one in which we are unaware of the outcome, reluctance to change may block the way. When we stop doing what we have always done, life becomes different. It is an adventure we must take to enrich our lives.

Be open to signs, as signs are all around for you to notice and make the connection. Notice when the complexity of a dream, a song, or a visual cue all come together to tell you the same thing. Trust the natural rhythm of synchronicity in everything. Learn to trust the complimentary sets of synchronicities that illuminate the unknown path of your intuition.

Sometimes there are repeated messages. Repetition may indicate an important message. Repetition could help to overcome skepticism. Sometimes repeated messages confirm; "Yes, this is it." Other times repeated themes are a dire warning. Even when you think you have heard the message several times before, record it to keep track of when it occurs—if you are following it— and to determine its relevance. The simplest, most repetitive message could be the most profoundly relevant. Sometimes we choose to overlook what stares us down. The bold and blatantly in your face message may seem repulsive to those who reject the starkness of an intuitive message.

When in the presence of others or an environment or situation, do you ever feel a force pulling you closer or a strong aversion pushing you away? I usually have high regard for this feeling and avoid people, places, and situations when I feel "stay-away" energy.

I felt static as I listened to "Riders of the Storm" by The Doors[4]. I thought there was resistance. When I ignored the feeling, the message came in another format, and I woke up that night with another message. A static electricity storm occurs when we are on different frequencies. Charge and friction create a strong elemental connection. The static attraction could become magnetic, but be cautious of the storm.

If only I had listened to my intuition and heeded the warning. Intuition told me all that I needed to know. Be

[4] The Doors. (1971). "Riders of the Storm." *L.A. Woman.* Elektra Records.

cautious of the storm! With fierce determination, I entered an emotional storm that could have been avoided. This environment had a strong negative attractor quality. In one way, it pushed me away; in another, I was drawn right into static resistance. Quickly, I recognized that my intuition was correct, and I vacated the storm. Since this experience, I now trust intuition to guide the way and avoid unnecessary storms.

Think of a time when you recognized and chose to ignore your intuition. What happened?

What are some challenges you encounter when listening to your intuition? Have you disregarded nightmares as meaningless? How do you realize what is meaningful? Do you question that nagging feeling? Do you wish that song would get out of your head already? Are you wondering why you keep having the same dream? Perhaps you recognize the signs but are unsure of their meaning. Do you assume it's unimportant? Do you resist your intuition? Do you want things to go the way that you direct? Do you know that you know and yet want another sign of confirmation? Sometimes you may receive confirmation that has nothing to do with the context. Do you disregard the inspired coincidence? Do you wonder where to begin?

The activities in the chapters ahead will provide the opportunity to take small action steps to overcome all these challenges. The action steps will be subtle and nonthreatening components of easily applicable activities. This gentle approach will assist you in accessing your wild intuition.

The Vault

Intuition is subtle and fleeting. When you ignore intuition long enough, your life may become a nightmare. Nightmares can become indistinguishable from reality. I had a nightmare that I was trapped inside a bank vault with three men holding guns. The men wanted to take the wealth. I thought *You couldn't rob anything if we were all trapped inside. The oxygen would become depleted, and we would all suffocate.*

When you keep the wealth of your intuition trapped within, it becomes locked within a vault. Holding back creates tension that closes your mind and dulls your senses. Putting blocks and hurdles in the way doesn't keep you or anyone else safe. We suppress our intuition when we go against our natural warning system. Suppressing intuition generates tension within the body. The blocks and obstacles will extend beyond the moment and close the vault. When you resist, you reject your intuition. Sense where in your body you feel the resistance. The more frequently you reject your intuition, the more interference you put in the way of allowing your intuition to navigate peacefully.

Go beyond your limited mental bounds. By removing the obstacles, you can realize your full potential. We can perceive infinite possibilities and excel with unlimited potential when we open the vault and allow energy to circulate freely.

Intuition is supportive and protective. Allow energy to flow to become attuned to inner peace. Create a warm, welcoming space where you feel relaxed and open to receiving. Become comfortable and receptive in this nurturing space to allow intuition to come naturally. Open and relax the mind, body, and emotional centers. Be mentally and spiritually present and allow the occurrence. Relax and let the tension leave the body. Resistance fades away. Inner calmness permeates in waves and ripples. Peace transcends into universal harmony. Allowing your energy to flow freely will allow your intuition to thrive.

Right now, you are surrounded by all the resources you require. Imagine the ease of following your intuition to have a fun free-flowing experience. Intuition is at its peak when you are involved in a new adventure: when you have experienced something new in your life and applied your strengths and knowledge to navigate successfully.

Intuition thrives on your natural abilities. You will use your strengths to access your wild intuition. Cultivating strong intuitive senses helps you to navigate. Allow intuitive thoughts, sensations, emotions, and vibrations to drive your actions. Trust that the guidance is meant for you to live your best life.

Consider what thoughts, feelings, and actions were taken when you experienced something new. How did you feel when you last visited a place you'd never been to before? How did you learn a new skill? How did you become familiar when you began a new job? How did you feel when you experienced a new relationship? Were you excited? Were you scared? What went well? How will you use what worked in the past to succeed in the present time?

Growth

Spring in the northeast is a time of transition from a cold dormant state to a season of growth and awakening. Spring begins with freezing temperatures, snow, and ice. As time progresses, the temperature increases and the snow slowly melts. Eventually, the crocus begins to bloom and leaves start to bud on the trees. Animals awaken from hibernation. In time, the warmth stays, and daylight remains longer. Like the spring season, representing a time of growth, your creative awareness will grow, and your wild intuition will awaken.

Embrace this time with lively acceleration toward positive insights on the horizon. Transition into a new beginning of discovery. We are more receptive to intuition when we are in a new experience. Be open to exploring and having new experiences. Look forward to the adventure with excitement. Intuition does not follow an established routine to achieve expected results. Unexpected things happen along the way. Creativity and freedom exist in the unknown. Uncertainty is part of the process of discovery. Stay open and embrace the unknown. Life becomes interesting when you follow your curiosity. Approach life with a new level of curiosity. Be aware of clues. Signs will come in many forms. Allow the mystery of intuition to show the way. Actively engage with your surroundings. Learn how to make meaningful connections among unrelated things. Keep evolving, learning, changing beliefs, and increasing knowledge. With practice, recognizing intuition becomes easier. Build the foundation for intuitive discovery. Simple techniques make it easier to access your intuition as a guide for more significant life events.

Life is limitless. Your connection with the world around you will broaden as you explore and find new meaning in your everyday surroundings. Intellectual and perceptual knowledge will expand beyond the boundaries of your current level of recognition. Allow expansive perceptual openness to occur as you awaken your wild intuition.

Chapter 3:

Creative Awareness

The adventure begins in a state of creative awareness. The applicable definition of the concept is as follows. **Creative awareness is a state of being alert, open, calm, and perceptive**. Inner calmness allows you to be more alert. You must be open to receiving intuitive information. Being perceptive will enhance your ability to make new connections between internal and external stimuli.

Creative awareness is a level of alertness in which life becomes a new beginning filled with wonder, curiosity, excitement, and awe. It is possible to experience a feeling of absolute connection to the world focused on capturing the moments and magnificence of your surroundings. When you are alert to the world in which we live, you notice things you would typically overlook. Awe promotes a sense of presence in which time fades away, and day-to-day concerns diminish. Time may feel altered as if hours pass by in microseconds, and life may have the most meaning. It is easy to establish a connection with natural surroundings. The experience of awe presents an opportunity for personal transformation. Awe inspires a greater level of openness, wonder, and desire to connect and provokes positive emotions.

To cultivate creative awareness, it is essential to have an open mind that allows for an expansive experience. The characteristics of openness are a welcoming attitude that accepts and entertains new information and experiences without judgment. It is essential not to limit your experiences as you have them. Open the space to move beyond the limitations of the mind to allow dynamic access to intuitive information. Your receptivity is enhanced. Openness generates the potential to receive. The level of openness will become apparent in the variety of adventures you will have.

An essential part of creative awareness is enhanced perception. This is achieved by being actively engaged in the present moment. Maximize the moment from wherever you are. Treat each moment as if it will be the only moment you will ever have of the experience you are having. Act as if this is the only moment you will ever have. Maximize the small amount of time that you have left in this life experience and give it the most heartfelt attention. This method of thinking invites depth of focus which expands perception. Be present and enjoy whatever you are doing in its entirety.

A calm approach invites a wealth of intuitive information. When you are calm, you are more receptive to intuition. Slow down. Pause, reflect, and be grateful for each moment. Maximize this moment with gratitude. Acknowledge that it is a special gift showcasing the majestic. Being calm allows for equanimity and neutral balance. This mindset allows more content and context to surface.

Be a Brave Adventurer

Intuition functions like a secret adventure map where there are paths, and you become curious to follow where they lead. The absence of a clearly defined map makes you receptive to divine direction. Be a brave adventurer. Trust that there are options along every path. Every road taken will always be the way. Focus on where you are going. The finished product, like artwork, may be unknown during the process but will be revealed upon completion. Follow it along, do it, make it, be it, and let it evolve into what it is meant to be. Just take a step and then another and allow the way to appear. Detach from a perceived outcome or timeline and recognize that this is a mysterious adventure. Step away from the familiar and embark on a journey of connection with the unknown. Move forward boldly as you find the way. Moving forward, adapting, and adjusting to living your best life are all made easier by intuition. Your intuition will support you in choosing action over reaction from a place of strength. Success is on the horizon.

You are the genius of your life. Access your brilliance on this deeply introspective journey. Creative awareness awakens your senses and serves as a force for new beginnings and active engagement in your life. Some things you notice will spark a warm sense of joy and excitement. An internal knowing of "Yes, this is it." This is confirmation of an intuitive message. Genuine self-confidence will grow as you welcome creative awareness and trust the adventure of your wild intuition.

The adventure involves many activities to develop creative awareness and awaken wild intuition. The more frequent and consistent your intuition becomes with practice, the more likely it is to lead the way to precognitive knowledge—becoming more alert, perceptive to senses, observant, and cognizant of the environment. Being in tune with the physical, sensory, and emotional cues in your body will enhance your recognition of internal intuitive information. Heightening your observational skills will allow access to intuitive information from the environment. This allows you to discover new meaning in your surroundings.

Activities to Help Recognize Intuition

- Learn how to ask open conceptual questions to get an intuitive answer.

- Discover answers from unexpected sources.
- Imagine viewing life from different perspectives.
- Learn how to break patterns.
- Develop focused observational skills to find what you didn't even know you were looking for.
- Receive significant intuitive guidance from the photos you take.
- Recognize greater meaning and inspiration from your pictures.
- If a song comes into your mind at random, follow the lyrics to find out what it's trying to say.
- Discover if there is a soundtrack foreshadowing your life.
- Listen to music as a new source of meaning and inspiration.
- Create metaphors and analogies as you discover and reveal your deepest thoughts and feelings.
- Generate poetic and sometimes prophetic statements while practicing intuitive writing.
- Reveal ways to recognize messages in dreams.
- Determine how your dreams connect to your life.
- Learn how to overcome recurrent nightmares and the terror of sleep paralysis.

As you go through this book, blend some of the activities:

- Go on a photo journey to a place where you feel a geographic connection.
- When you ask a question, find the answer in the lyrics of a song.
- Create a metaphor while appreciating nature.

Wander and admire the beauty and elegance of the world around you. Explore, knowing that adventure will find you. Connect with your wild in the most unexpected places.

It's time to let the wild out!

Chapter 4:

Sensory Engagement

The earth generates sound and vibration in the rocks, the rippling of the water, the crashing of waves, and the leaves rustling in the wind. After receiving a sound healing, I became more acutely aware of the sounds. I spent the rest of the day at Lido Beach and experienced the beach in a way I had never before. I could hear the roar of the waves in the tone of "Om" and the wind in the sky in the tone of "Woo." As I lay on the white quartz sand, I could hear the sound of the sand blowing in the wind. This experience was as magical as it was bizarre and unique, and it ended perfectly with a rainbow over the sun at sunset over the Gulf of Mexico.

The senses provide clues and intuitive information. Develop awareness of your senses to access the intuitive knowledge that they provide.

Take a moment to practice this activity to become alert to the sensory, emotional, and physical information available:

- Focus attention on any sensory, emotional, or physical body sensations.
- Learn your most substantial intuitive feelings.
- Determine which of your senses provides the most potent information.
- Which sensations call your attention? Ask what they indicate.
- What is this feeling here to tell you?
- Your insights have ways of communicating with you. Determine what they reveal.
- What is your body telling you that your mind must recognize and act upon?
- Where from the entire body do you feel it deep within your soul?
- Where does it come from?
- What is it calling upon you to do?

The purpose of this activity is to slow down and engage all your senses to become attentive to recognize the information available from within. Activate and engage the senses as you perceive the environment. Ask questions about what you sense to increase your perception of sensory intuition.

Sensory Awareness Action Steps:

- What do you see?
  - What is a question that this sight evokes?
- What sounds do you hear?
  - What comes to mind when listening?
- What do you smell?
  - What does the scent make you wonder about?
- What do you taste?
  - What does the taste imply?
- What do you feel as you touch something?
  - What is surprising about the feeling?
- What physical sensation do you feel in your body?
  - What does the physical sensation indicate?
- What emotion do you feel?
  - What do your emotions suggest to you?
  - Notice what bodily sensations you feel from the emotion.
  - Where in your body does the emotion originate?

The above technique could be personalized as you ask your own questions about the sensory information you acknowledge. Apply this technique with activities in later chapters to expand your sensory experience in a variety of settings. Build the foundation of sensory awareness.

Physical and emotional sensations are meant to provide information. Both positive and negative feelings serve as indicators. The senses could indicate the appropriate action or the necessity to change direction. Good feelings may be a sign to keep going. Moments of heightened emotional intensity are meant to reveal the way to guide you forward into a new adventure. Bad feelings may indicate a signal to stop, find another route, or proceed cautiously with alertness to potential dangers. The information may serve as a cautionary tale directing you on a totally different path. Emotions get in the way when they strike intensely and overshadow the intuitive information present. These are the moments when some external situation causes a full-body emotional response to overtake you. The physical response of fear might cause sweaty palms, shaky legs, and butterflies, along with unproductive thoughts entering your mind. When you are aware of the emotion, you may change it.

Numerical Scuba Breathing

The physiological state can be changed into a calm emotional and physical state with the application of numerical scuba breathing. To enter a relaxed physical state, practice numerical scuba breathing to release emotions and thoughts and allow energy to flow. When scuba breathing, I inhale longer, slower, deeper breaths and exhale longer, slower, deeper breaths. I never hold my breath and try to exhale slightly longer than I inhale.

This technique helps me relax, release any tension, and breathe at a steady rhythmic pace.

Computational math focuses the mind on cognitive thinking, disrupting the emotional mind and ruminating thought patterns. Math distracts your thoughts and breaks the focus on your emotional state. Once you feel relaxed, ruminating thoughts fade away. As you begin this technique, you may be unable to inhale or exhale for the total count; with practice, your breathing capacity will increase. If you lose track of the numbers and math, keep going and make up a number sequence. Once you feel calm, the technique has been successful. This could be done silently or out loud.

Numerical Scuba Breathing Action Steps:

- Inhale slowly as you count: 2 plus 2 is 4 plus 4 is 8 plus 8 is 16 plus 16 is 32
- Exhale slowly as you count: 2 plus 2 is 4 plus 4 is 8 plus 8 is 16 plus 16 is 32
- Continue each set at least four times
- Alternately, try chanting "Woo" on the inhale and "Om" on the exhale.

This activity works well at the onset of a heightened emotional response where you need to quickly disengage. Identify the emotion as it occurs to slow your response so that you may choose to enter a calm state. As soon as you have released the emotion, you may regain productive focus. Recognize the message in the emotion from a calm state.

Driving in the Snowstorm

I was driving in a lake-effect snowstorm; visibility was reduced by blowing and drifting snow, causing white-out conditions. I could feel fear and anxiety, which triggered thoughts of what if another car was coming and we collided. What if I go off the road? What if I am driving into worse conditions? This road is across a hilltop; how will I drive down the hill safely? I recognized those thoughts were generated in response to the emotional mind. I realized that driving in snowy weather triggers my emotional mind.

I know that I'm driving cautiously. I listen to music and sing along with the lyrics to minimize my emotions. I think about the genre of the music being reggaeton, and I think of being on vacation in a warm location. The heat in the car is set at 80, and I feel warm. I think of being on vacation. If this were a sandstorm I was driving in rather than a snowstorm, I would feel the excitement and think of the experience as a great adventure. I would consider the experience to be a once-in-a-lifetime adventure, a fantastic tale to tell, and something that would make me want to stop driving and take pictures in the storm.

My son, who has been peacefully reading a book about wolves, suddenly looks up and says, "They are in a blizzard in my book, and we are in one. This is cool."

Our perceptions and ability to regulate our emotion-based reactions are fundamental to our success in situations. If I had reacted to fear-based thoughts, I would have reduced my cognitive ability to drive home safely and dulled my receptivity to intuitive information, which could be crucial in a situation like this.

Emotion in Music

Listening to music may provoke various emotions. Music may assist you in becoming aware of your emotions and changing your emotional state. In the example above, I used music to change an emotional state. I was feeling fear, but the reggaeton genre excites me, so I chose to reframe fear into excitement. When you are aware of the impact of music on your emotions, you can use that to your advantage. Being in tune with the emotion of the music may change your perception of an incident. Determine the effect of different music on your emotions in the following activity.

Emotion in Music Action Steps:

- Listen to a song.
- What emotion do you feel from the instruments or tone of voice?
- What emotion is incited by the lyrics?

- What emotion do you feel from the genre?
- How would you apply music to improve your emotional response to a situation?

This exercise is to help you become more conscious of your emotional state.

Practice this activity with music from differing genres. Try applying music to enhance or alter an emotional experience. As you work with the music, you begin to awaken your musical intuition.

Emotional Reframe

When we know our emotional state, we can use the dynamic information to take appropriate actions or allow unproductive emotional states to lead the way.

You may also evaluate the emotion to determine the intuitive message. What does the emotion call to your attention? If you have heightened awareness of your emotional state, you may reduce your emotion-based response. Reframe the emotion to deal with the situation from a cognitive perspective. To distance yourself, engage the cognitive part of the brain by asking yourself what is really going on here. Emotional states can be assessed, interpreted, and changed in the moment and in retrospect. There are also times when emotional states linger in rumination. When emotions stick and circulate, causing ruts, they could prevent the reception of intuition.

I was having lunch with a group of people at a conference. One woman talked about becoming angry and did not want to feel this way. I shared how to reframe the experience to disengage from the emotion at the moment.

Later in the day, I was approached by several people asking me to share the technique. It had worked so well for the woman at lunch that she mentioned her success with the application to others, and they wanted to know how to apply it. She employed this method:

Emotional Reframe Action Steps:

- View the situation as if you are no longer a part of the event.
- Imagine it as if you were watching characters perform the event.
- Change the characters to an animated version.
- Fast-forward the movements of the characters.
- Distort the voices until they are inaudible.
- Imagine you are farther away from the characters and the event.
- You are entirely removed from the action.

Next time you see this character or think of the event, imagine the sequence you created. This character has become hilarious and no longer affects your emotions.

Use these action steps to distance yourself in moments of adversity as well. Apply the technique to disengage from the interaction by imagining that you are watching characters perform and you are not one of the actors. This technique assists in placing an emotional distance to prevent becoming consumed by emotion during a current adverse event. Emotional memories may be changed to prevent a block of free-flowing energy. Practice the technique to release the stagnant or dominant emotion interfering with the joy of the present.

If we are stuck continuously replaying an adverse event, it blocks the path forward as we are no longer focused on where we are going. Our focus is directed toward where we were. Replaying the past in memory may prevent the recognition of intuition in the present. When free of emotional blocks, we become receptive to fully experiencing all the present has to offer.

Chapter 5:

Geographic Connection

Have you ever arrived at a place and been suddenly transported to another place in time? I was hiking in a shale rock creek in the woods of Western New York when I came upon a vortex between the past, present, and impending future. It was a historical review—a fantasy about traveling back in time to a memory of a fateful meeting. I encountered the exact location where my life took an entirely different course and changed forever. A strange phenomenon overtook me. Time felt altered while in this place. My mind and body were completely consumed by this time loop. The water was soothing, and the sound of the waterfalls distracted any thoughts. I took a picture to showcase the current time, which was a long time ago.

If you could return to a location where your life changed, would you? What would you do while you were there? How would that change your thoughts about where you are? Would you enter into a time vortex as I did? Many years after visiting that location, I realized that it was a place that ignited my intuition. And I wonder what influence that had on the dramatic change in my life all those years ago.

There are places where your intuition is most acute. There may be specific geographic places where your intuition thrives. Some areas may entice you, drawing you in, while others may repel you, warning you to stay away. People, places, and situations all emit an energetic feeling that can be either an attractor pulling you in or a repellant indicating to stay away. Consider your elemental connections in the following activity. Choose a place and go there to practice this activity.

Elemental Connection Action Steps:

- What do you sense from the environment?
- What is the feel of the place?
- Do you feel a connection to the rocks?
- What do you think about the plants?
- Does water provide a sensory link?
- What elements are you most drawn to?
  - How do you describe the feeling of attractors?
  - Where in your body do you feel the attraction?
- Which elements repel you?

- o How do you describe the feeling of repellants?
- o Where in your body do you feel the repellant?

The purpose of this activity is to assist you in becoming familiar with your connection to the natural environment. Practice this activity in various locations to determine your strongest elemental connections. Where do you experience either attractors or repellants? What happens when you listen to them? What about when you choose to ignore them? Becoming attuned to your personal attractors and repellants pulls you into alignment within and with the environment. Align with your center where your wild is brightest and most intense.

Notice the attractors that pull you in. I feel the attractors as light, as if I am pure energy without a body and have merged with the place. Time feels slow and goes by very quickly. My senses are heightened and alert—processing more information than usual. It is an exotic, sometimes erotic, feeling of connection. The upcoming story about Allan Gardens and the previous story about Lido Beach showcase what happens when I connect with a place.

Lido Beach is a place where I access my intuition. Long before ever visiting there, I was shown the place in my dreams where I saw a white sand beach with shells leading to a pine forest with pinecones and then to a mangrove forest. I also saw this place while meeting with a psychic for a reading. What are the places that frequent your dreams and connect you with your intuition?

Beware of any feelings of repellant or stay-away forces. I encounter repellants as unexpected coldness in an atmosphere, sudden and lasting coldness of my hands, a sense of fog in my mind, or a draining type of feeling that takes my energy away. It's a feeling where the space feels so dark that it's difficult to feel anything beyond the stern, cold darkness. It's as if an invisible fence keeps me from going closer. Jerome, Arizona, and other historical sites have provoked this feeling. Where are the places that you choose to stay away from?

The elements and places that most connect with your intuition will also arrive in dreams. I am most drawn to the warm coastal locations with turquoise water and white sand, as well as the extreme heat of the desert with red rock slot canyons and red sand. The turquoise water comes in many forms in my dreams with intuitive messages. I frequently dream of the desert. Because I am aware of the connection to my intuition, I pay attention to dreams with these elements and am alert and open to receiving messages in this format. These places provoke some of my most substantial intuitive experiences. Become attentive to the prompt reception of messages in these places that most heighten your intuition. You may also be mindful that there may be a message if you dream about these places.

The subaquatic riverscapes are a strong intuitive geographic attractor, with the sound of the water and the vibration of the rocks attracting me. I dreamt that I was in a landslide with snow-covered trees in New Zealand. I followed the direction of the flow to a newly created waterfall. I couldn't go back because the path was gone. Deep turquoise water went in both directions, leading to the waterfall or out to sea. I could not stay at the bottom of the waterfall or frozen at the top of the landslide. Boulders were floating and going upstream. The intuitive message arrived. "Go with the momentum, and you'll land exactly where you belong. Momentum will take you where you are meant to go. There is no longer a map because the territory has changed. Chart a new course. Your past is not your future. The landslide shows there is no turning back now. Go forward by following the reverse flow of the water. Follow the path before it is gone. The water generates more momentum and power as it flows in reverse." We are meant to flow back to get to what is intended to be manifested.

In retrospect, it came to my awareness that this was a precognitive dream. The summer after the dream, I went hiking with friends along the Niagara River from Devil's Hole State Park to Whirlpool State Park. One friend compared the hike to his adventures in New Zealand. Five hours, eight miles, and hundreds of stairs later, we had the finest day and stories to tell that strengthened the bonds of our new friendships. The hike was longer because some stairs were out, and safety workers were rappelling on the rocks to practice rescue techniques which caused rockfall areas. We walked against the river's flow along large boulders. We navigated the delays and became certified rock balancers while adapting to changing terrain and river conditions. This hike led to HypnoThoughts Live in Las Vegas and a rigorous hike in a flooded red rock slot canyon in Zion National Park. HypnoThoughts Live is where I heard about the course that taught me how to publish this book, and that was what was meant to be manifested.

Go to the places where you are drawn to and experience what happens. A young man with so much excitement for all that life offers recently asked me how to narrow down and choose what experiences to have in life.

I replied, "Try everything that interests you and then decide if it is something you want to do again."

As you try everything, you will go beyond your current level of awareness and get to what is meant to be manifested. As you try things, they will lead to other things you didn't even know about. Follow the path on a journey of natural discovery. Have fun as you experience everything.

Geographic Connection Action Steps:

- Go to a location where you feel inspired.

- Activate your senses with the Sensory Awareness Action Steps.

- Ask a question about what you want guidance on.

- What do you recognize?

- What do your senses indicate?

- What message do you receive?

This technique is meant to help you expand your intuition by connecting with a place that naturally activates it. Your intuition will intensify when you connect with the places that naturally connect with you.

Chapter 6:

Nature Admiration

Ghost Pond

While observing my son fishing at Ghost Pond, I discovered a broken rock. The rock was beige on the outside and green quartz on the inside. I wrote about my observations and other thoughts that entered my mind. "Take the time to look at what's inside. Inquire and get to know about the beauty within." A turtle surfaced. "We have only touched the surface. There is an unknown world in the depth of the water." It submerged when it recognized me. I assumed the turtle chose fear and swam away. "Turn fear into fascination. The turtle will return to take another breath and peer once again. The turtle is back to sustain life."

I hear and feel loud sound vibrations in the railroad tracks. "There are peaceful opportunities. Appreciate the harmony of life. Allow the universe's delicate balance and energetic pull to determine the time. Be open, transparent, and receptive. Have undaunted, relentless hope, optimism, love, exquisite tenderness, and gentleness. Stop thinking and feel the moment. We are at a crossing: yield and follow the indicators and slowly proceed around the curve, up a slight hill to an unknown horizon that awaits. Enjoy the mystery and live life with passion."

The example above was an enjoyable opportunity to connect more deeply with the natural environment. The stimuli enriched my thought process bringing new thoughts to mind.

Walking outside in nature allows for a quiet, curiously contemplative experience. Nature calms the mind and increases creativity through a sense of awe. Nature provokes an innate sense of curiosity. Wonder how the organisms respond to one another. Ask questions. Use your instincts, imagination, and freedom of thought to appreciate living systems. Recognize the beneficial relationships and interactions as the organisms work together. Where do you fit within the environment? Organisms adapt to their environmental conditions. How do they thrive in various situations? Observe everything around you with intrinsic curiosity. Recognize the details of the environment, such as the organisms, the weather conditions, the amount of water, and light. Collect the details and perceptions you have made through your encounters with the world. Consider every detail of the environment as significant. Learn from what you observe. Actively value your encounters and apply natural intelligence to your life.

Because the natural world provides a wealth of information, this section is divided into multiple activities. You may focus on one section independently or apply all sections together in your observation. Find a place outside in nature to explore. This might be your backyard, a local park, or any area with natural elements. Bring a notebook. Relax and calm your mind. Awaken and engage your senses. Spend as much time as is necessary concentrating on your surroundings. Observe and capture as much detail as possible. Take it all in. Pay close attention to all that surrounds you. Write about your observations and impressions. Freely write about anything that arrives in your mind while you are here. Write about your insights and motivations.

Nature Admiration Action Steps:

- Practice sensory awareness.
    - What do you see?
    - What do you feel?
    - What do you hear?
- How has nature inspired you?
- What messages come to your mind?

Admire Life Action Steps:

- Observe an animal.
  - How does the animal interact with the environment?
  - What information do you receive from this animal?
- What do you notice about the trees, plants, or other living things around you?
- What message do you receive from the trees, plants, and other living organisms?

Atmosphere Interaction Action Steps:

- Feel the warmth and catch the light radiating from the sun.
- What is illuminated by the sun?
- Where do you see rays of sunlight or shadows?
- It is nighttime; what do you see in the night sky?
- What do you hear among the sounds of the night?

Ecosystem Appreciation Action Steps:

- What relationships do you notice in the environment?
- What connections do you make?
- What characteristics do you observe?
- What patterns do you recognize?
- What colors and textures do you find?

- What has shaped the environment? Was it created by the pressure of the wind or flowing water?
- What else do you notice?
- What interests you?
- List your thoughts about the experience.

Nature is a platform for intuitive insights to be revealed. Humans evolved in nature over time, and by going back into nature, new insights will appear. Time in nature provides an opportunity to explore your instincts. A fresh perspective may be ignited as you go out into nature. Pay attention to the present moment as you explore the world around you. Take the time to appreciate nature. Find meaning in your interactions with the natural world. Energize as you connect with nature and awaken your intuition.

Explore without a destination. Enter with the mindset of wanting to be surprised. Know that you will see what you didn't know you were looking for. Every element tells a story. What story do you see? Learn from what you have in front of you. It's a mysterious adventure, and you never know what you may find.

Three Example Applications

A man participating in one of my workshops noticed all the danger signs. The signs indicated "Keep Out," "Do Not Enter," and "Caution." At first, he felt like he was being told what to do and that the place was dangerous based on all the signs. As he continued to walk and observe the signs, he realized that the signs were there to protect the citizens and keep everyone safe. The signs were a guide to the safest path. In a group discussion, he shared that he works with trauma victims and will incorporate this activity to help victims discover the safety factors that protect them.

At a university, a participant identified as a perfectionist and decided to find imperfections during one of the activities. Upon completion, she was excited to share that she found perfection in the seemingly imperfect things in life. What led her to this discovery was taking a picture of a sink drain and realizing that the person who installed it took the time to line the screws up perfectly with the design of the holes in the drain. The care and precision that went into this changed her view, and she felt that the drain was a work of art and perfection.

At an art gallery, a participant shared how she observed student artwork in which the student made several drawings of pillowcases folded in various ways. She was intrigued by the attention to detail in the drawings and the way the artist must have spent a significant amount of time folding and observing the creases to create the drawing. The connection she made from her observations to her own life was that she feels like she is always in a hurry rushing from one thing to another. Observing the artist's experience reminded her of her desire to slow down and appreciate what she is doing.

Admire a place you frequent to practice everyday observation. Perhaps you live in a city. The city streets provide bright signs and stimuli that may correlate, generating a complex story of answers. City streets offer bright, colorful lights and a variety of words and graphics to observe that may provide intuitive messages. The combination of elements may interact to tell a story. The architectural designs add characteristics to define the space. Notice signs, words, graphics, lights, people, and unexpected nature. Every place has its own unique story. Inspirational words and exciting content are everywhere. Interact with the variety of elements and make your individual interpretation. What will you discover?

Everyday Observation Action Steps:

- Choose any location.
- Observe the environment.
- Look at the architecture, the décor, the people.
- Hear the music.
- Read the words on the signs.
- Photograph what interests you.
- Take notes on what you observe.
- How does this experience relate to your life?
- Make connections between your observations and your thoughts.

After engaging in this activity, you'll be inspired to adopt a fresh perspective on the world. Something will spark your interest. Enjoy the colors, the scents, the variety, and the diversity of the environment. The action steps could occur in any location, whether inside your home or in a public space. Discover new meanings wherever you are.

The techniques in this chapter assist you in broadening your thought perspectives to access intuitive information beyond your standard thought patterns. Taking the time to appreciate nature and practice everyday observation opens your receptivity to accessing new knowledge as you acknowledge the things you may typically overlook. When you enhance your observational skills, you expand the variety of your thinking. Connect with yourself and the world with your senses open, actively alert, and attuned to stimuli, ready to receive enlightenment. The combination of physical, emotional, environmental, and experiential information expands receptivity to comprehend multi-faceted interactive intuitive messages. Be receptive and allow the graceful union of your intellect and intuition.

Chapter 7:

Questions That Answer

D o you ever ask a question hoping that an answer will magically appear? Whenever I do this, the answers will appear right in front of me, no matter where I am. I have always believed that adventure would find me, and it always does.

You can get the response you need if you ask the correct question. Strive to develop open-ended questions to receive the most dynamic response. Open-ended questions allow for many possibilities to emerge, preventing the mind from seeking a particular predetermined answer. The more open-ended the question, the better. This type of question asks for more than "Yes" or "No." It asks how to, how might, or what are the ways. The objective is to invite explanatory answers. To receive the best level of intuitive solution without the influence of your mind driving the outcome, ask about the general concept rather than about a specific result. What question to ask? Open-ended, simple, and highlights what you want to know without providing an answer to the question. If the answer is unclear, ask "What does this mean?" If you want to know why then ask "Why?" Here are some examples of questions:

Powerful questions:

- What information do I need to know?
- What do I need to recognize?
- What are the hidden factors?
- What information will propel me forward?
- What other ways are there?
- How might I fulfill my potential in the best way?
- What are my best next steps?
- What is the best direction to proceed?
- What is the best action to take toward_____?

When you want to know yes or no on a particular outcome, ask yes or no questions. Refrain from seeking to see the words "Yes" or "No." Allow what you see to provide a more descriptive answer. This method will give you more than a yes or no answer and describe the answer's reason. This method is unlike flipping a coin and leaving the matter to chance. As you discover the reason for the yes or no message, it will provide additional confirmation of the message beyond random chance. Alternately, try to go beyond yes or no questions by developing a question that asks about what's causing you to ask yes or no questions. You may just find the answer within your own question.

For example, I went on a first date. He was interested, and I felt uncertain about even going on a second date. I consulted the tarot cards four separate times to assess the potential. Three times I drew the devil and once the death card. The cards were a definitive no and indicated that disaster would follow. I never went on a second date.

There are many ways to find the answer to your questions. Here are a few suggestions. Ask a question when practicing any of the activities in this book. Consult tarot or oracle cards if you have them. Look at the pictures to see the answer. Read a random page of a book to find the answer. Look within or search the environment on a quest for the solution in external stimuli. You may find the answer within or out there or a combination of both within and out there. The following activities will show you how to find the answer within and out there.

Finding the Answer Within

Ask a question and write the answers. You may find the answers within your thoughts. If you write what comes into your mind, you will find that you already have the answer.

I asked, "What action can I take to make my dreams real?" I wrote: "Stay positive and focused. Reach out to friends. Ask mentors for help. Give energy to aspirations. Pay attention to the song lyrics that come into my mind. Do things my way. Write my book. Develop my content: words and pictures and short reflective paragraphs. Spend time with people who elevate me and let go of those who bring me down."

I love the beach and the desert.

I asked a follow-up question. "What will bring me to the beach and the desert?"

Prioritize what is important. Decide what you want. Ask for it. Be prepared for what you receive.

The fascinating part about the answer is that I went to both the beach and the desert soon after writing that. At the time of the writing, there were no plans in place. I presented at a conference by the beach and attended a conference in the desert. It all came together naturally without much thought or planning.

The Answer is Out There

You may find the answer by asking a question and finding the solution by observing your environment. I was feeling stuck in my life and waiting at the airport for a delayed flight exaggerated the feeling. I contemplated a question. "How to get unstuck?"

The answer: "I am creating my happiness. Love is the strongest emotion, and that's why it's so powerful. When it comes to achievement and motivation, pursue my passion without boundaries. Boundaries block progress and create conflicting forces against growth. Push past that stuck block in pursuit of doing what I love without boundaries. That is how I break free; it's love."

The answer came within the random pages of books and magazines and in the random thoughts that entered into my mind. I ignored the titles of the books and magazines and any references to advertising. I didn't want to get distracted by them because that's not the point of this exercise. The point is to catch what meaning speaks to you in the moment about what you want to know. Continue on and take note of something new if you are still searching for the solution. It is entirely up to you where you go on this adventure.

Write the message as it occurs because intuition is fleeting, especially when you are busy with many distractions. Take notes to document what you observe before the concept is lost. The ideas may be choppy initially as the story unfolds. The answer will be revealed later. Many times, there are several things that you will notice that tie together to generate the message. Keep the message in a contemporaneous journal. Save the original content. Years later, look back at the message you received. You may notice a new message as time goes on.

The airport message was more prevalent upon reflection. I read notes that I had taken at the International Meeting on Simulation in Healthcare

Conference and an academic paper that I had written at the time about emotional intelligence.

The question: "How to get unstuck?"

The answer: "Keep momentum by doing what I love."

I was a graduate student at the time, conducting an independent study on emotional intelligence and developing strategies to increase emotional intelligence. Naturally, in those days, a message about emotion would speak to me in a way that I would understand and heed the application. Even as I wrote about the airport message several years after receiving it, I was provided with new insight and awareness. When I read that message while writing this book, I felt good because I'm writing about what I love, and I know that I won't get stuck because I'm pursuing my passion.

You will receive the messages in a way that makes sense to you and strikes a chord with you. For me, love resonates with loud and clear messages from a reference point of an inner flame and intense passion that guides the way. Love is my guidepost. As you discover and apply your intuitive strengths, the messages will also be loud and clear for you. The more you recognize your intuitive guideposts, the more you will know that you have received intuitive messages as guidance on your path.

Finding the Answer Within AND Out There

You may find the answer in a blend of internal and external interactions of thoughts and stimuli. I contemplated how to proceed while walking around the Allan Gardens Conservatory in Toronto, Canada. The gardens were so beautiful and captivating that I was no longer actively contemplating the question of how to proceed. I loved the gardens and felt absolute awe and wonder as if I had entered a dream. I just wanted to stay there forever.

I spent a long time in the cactus room, viewing the familiar with the thought that this is all there is. Then I entered another room and took many photos from the underside of the leaves, looking up toward the light and capturing the close magnified details. I felt awe, wonder, and excitement as I entered the next room. I felt blown away by the beauty and magnificence of the full bloom of the flowers. The exquisite immersive experience completely engulfed me in a state of awe.

The answer arrived while I was no longer thinking about the question. "There is no need to stay with the familiar or overanalyze every detail. Stop overanalyzing the past and explore the future. Take steps forward, and it will bloom how it's meant to and be unimaginably impressive. If we nurture what we love, it will grow and blossom and be sustainable over the long term."

Suddenly, having lost track of time, the gardens were about to close. I didn't want to leave.

A man responded, "It's okay; you can come back tomorrow."

His reply also answered my question. I felt a calm sense of warmth and joy, an internal knowing that I could always return to the beautiful garden.

Explore and discover the answer to your questions in the following action steps. This activity applies to finding answers within, out there, or when you have no questions at all. If you want to practice the activity without a question, skip the first step to explore and let adventure find you.

Questions That Answer Action Steps:

- What is it that you want guidance on? Ask a question.
- Enter a state of creative awareness: alert, open, calm, and perceptive.
- Choose a location to explore.
- Let adventure find you.
- Observe anything that appeals to you.
- Take notes of what enters your awareness as it occurs.
- Write the answer you receive.

After the observation, add your thoughts and what you think the meaning might be. Do not judge or alter the original presentation. Look at previous notes to see connections to the message. Consider the value of repeated themes in what you notice as they have messages. What do they indicate? What insights have you received? Keep the message for future reference.

Ask a question each day to strengthen this method of receiving answers. The more you explore and learn, the more answers will immerge. Allow curiosity to keep you questioning. Ask questions of value, meaning, and choice. Seek knowledge. Questions reveal possibilities yet to be considered. Questions enhance perspectives about what is possible. Allow for flexibility in the answers that appear. The message may come in an unexpected format.

Sometimes you look for confirmation, and you will find it. Other times, you have no idea what you seek, and it will find you. It is possible to receive an answer to a question you didn't even ask. For example, I heard an owl while outside with my dog one night. Then an owl flew to a window in the movie I was watching. Next, I saw an article about the discovery of a new species of owl. These occurrences were independent and were not influenced by the algorithms on a technical device. Owls do not frequent my awareness regularly. A quick check on owl symbolism revealed that owls symbolize intuition. I was writing this book about intuition, and it confirmed my intention to share with others how to access wild intuition.

The most important thing is to have an open mind and allow the information to present itself. Answer the door of opportunity. Intuitive answers provide the best next steps. Trust that the answer you receive is in your best interests. When you naturally allow the message, you will receive profound universal guidance that may stay with you for years.

Chapter 8:

Photo Journey

I magine as if. Wherever you are, you can step into the perspective of a different role in life and connect with intuitive feelings by engaging deeply with whatever is present. Follow the activity in the next paragraph to change your viewpoint multiple times. You will become aware of new insights into intuitive discovery as you change your perspective.

Imagine as if you are viewing a walking stick insect on a pine tree. You have never seen a walking stick bug in real life before. What specifics do you notice as you watch this gorgeous creature in person? And then, you notice a path illuminated by the sun. How do you feel about moving along this path? Where does that path take you? Your intuition has a message; what does it indicate? Walk beyond the forest and exit the path. You are under the sea among the coral and the fish. You feel the current and the warmth of the sun. Imagine as if you are this fish or this coral.

Why did you choose what you chose? What is your experience as this being? How does it feel to be a part of this ocean ecosystem? Your intuition provides another clue as you appreciate your connection with the natural world. What is the clue?

Now you leave the ocean and enter the sky. Imagine as if you have a bird's-eye view and you are soaring between land and sea. What do you see? Where are you going? Imagine viewing a surfer on top of the waves, feeling the sea's strengths and freedom and propelling force of flying through the air. What do you think as you watch the movement of the waves? You are flying above, viewing the waves and the rocks. What do you experience? What emotional insights have you encountered along the journey? What enters your mind? What messages are revealed as you complete the imaginary journey?

The purpose of this activity is to broaden your mindset through the appreciation of fantasy. As you explore another worldview beyond the everyday reality of life, you access the novelty—an essential aspect of creativity. When you view life from multiple viewpoints, you become aware of information and ways of thinking that you may typically overlook. The more expansive your view, the more novel connections and potential intuitive interactions you may encounter. Intuition is mystical. Explore going on a journey with a mind open to let adventure find and interact with you. Information and potential insights are everywhere, and you have to see them and make the applicable connection to your life.

In the opening to this chapter, you imagined scenic imagery. In the upcoming activities, you will view and take pictures from different perspectives.

Pictures are portals to another place at another time. Photos are moments frozen in time that allow you to step into an imaginary journey of remembering who you were and imagining who you want to become. Photos capture inspiration. Look within the images to find what is hidden within your soul. After you take a photo, take a moment to write an inspirational thought about what you observed. Generate a question that the image asks of you.

I snapped a photo of a flower and then made the observations listed below. It's meant to draw your attention deeply to the moment. "This bloom is temporary. Enjoy it for all its magnificence and color. It shall not last forever except in this snapshot of the eternal moment. The elusive forever encased within the images brought into the present from the past shall remain into the future. Life is frozen in a moment."

Each of us sees something different based on our mindset, life experiences, and where we are in our lives.

I have shared the image of a flower in workshops and asked others what the photo reveals. I suggested they view the world as if they were a flower and asked, "What is your experience as if you are the flower?" In one workshop, a participant reported seeing a fairy seated within the flower, and in the same workshop, one could smell the fragrance and hear bees approaching the flower. Another person could greatly appreciate the beauty of the flower. At the same time, another felt overwhelmed by the proximity of the photo to the flower, as if its treasure was overexposed. We may all be exposed to the same content; however, the context is open for unique individual interpretation.

Look at the cover of this book as you learn the technique. Imagine as if you are the wolf. What do you see through the eyes of the wolf? Where are you going in this terrain? What is your experience as the wolf? What information do you receive from the wolf? Now imagine as if you are falling snow. What do you feel as you descend from the sky and touch the trees? What does the snow reveal to you? Now you have become a part of the landscape. How does the landscape shape your life? What insights have you received from this journey?

Observe the pictures available to you to discover what they reveal to you. Practice the following activity with one of your pictures. Choose any image for this activity. This could be a picture you have taken or any other picture you want to look at.

Observe a Picture Action Steps:

- Find a picture to observe.
- Imagine if you were there in the picture right now.
- Where are you?
- How does the air feel?
- What sounds do you hear?
- What do you notice around you?
- What experience reminds you of this place?
- What does the image ask of you?
- What is your experience as the subject in the photo?
- What message is revealed within the photo?

This activity provides the opportunity to change your perspective. Photography provides a platform for observation and a change of perspective. A simple shift in perspective can spark new insights. Change perspective to change perception. Focus on perception and seeing things from various perspectives for a while. Look at life through a different lens.

Consider your experience with photography. Are you in the picture or the photographer? Think about when you take a picture. Why do you take pictures? Do you take photos to remember or to share on social media? What do you see that inspires you to take pictures? Look at a favorite photo you have taken. What did you experience at that moment? Why does that image resonate with you? What do you remember from that moment? What does this picture mean to you? Let's expand your photographic agenda and break the familiar pattern.

Taking pictures can expand your intuitive vision. To become more intuitive with photography, explore with the camera. Picture-taking is encouraged in any location. In the next activity, you will take pictures. Here are some ideas to shift perspectives while on the photo journey:

- Photograph new subjects from different angles.
- Look for patterns.
- Notice contrasts in the light or shadows.
- Observe combinations of subjects and focus on them.
- Take pictures of various colors.
- Capture macro or close-up images or landscapes farther away.
- Play with photographing moving objects.
- Take photos of things that you would not typically take pictures of, such as everyday things, imperfections, emotions, clutter, ordinary, industrial, oversized, repetitive, technological, spur of the moment, intriguing, mundane in a

new way, unrecognizable, blurred, shiny, dull, or seemingly unimportant.

- Focus on the elements below the surface, usually out of view, and photograph them.
- Decide on a theme—abstract, macro, shapes, or textures—and take a series of pictures.
- Take pictures through various lenses, such as different colored filters. The filters can be created by using transparent colored paper, a transparent object, or a fractal lens such as a kaleidoscope.

Photo Journey Action Steps:

- Apply any of the ideas in the paragraph above to get started.
- Focus on what interests you as you explore.
- Take lots of pictures.

Observe Your Images Action Steps:

- Select a photo you have taken.
- Focus for two minutes on the picture.
- What do you see?
- Write about your thoughts, feelings, and meaning behind the image.
- What is your experience as _____ (subject) in the photo?
- What does this subject ask of you?
- What is your answer?

- What does the subject tell you?
- What does this image represent?
- How will you use this photo in your daily life?
- What intuitive discoveries did you make?

This activity allows you to expand your observations beyond the moment. With a picture, you can spend more time on the details and magnify what you see. This allows for more time for reflection and introspection. Visual context stimulates conceptual thinking. The camera is a tool for you to savor the moment. As you inspect the image with depth, you may reveal hidden messages within the imagery and within yourself.

Photography inspires us to make life more beautiful. Take photos of the good times to remember what's good about being alive and to enjoy life. Focus on what's meaningful right where you are. Take an image of an important moment every day. Surround yourself with beautiful images to increase energy and positivity. Look at the pictures you have taken as a source of inspiration. Embrace the gift of photography as a way to see and express significant intuitive inspiration through appreciation of imagery. You can make a beautiful moment infinite.

Chapter 9:

Follow the Lyrics

Music unites us with divine genius. Music ignites our senses. Songs can fluently narrate our life experiences. A song can trigger a memory or an emotion. Music can spark intuitive awareness. Follow the music on the path of intuition.

Become more attentive to the music you hear to ignite your musical intuition. Expand your music selection to increase your musical intuitive reception. Notice the music on the radio, in movies, and as you walk into stores. When you hear a new or unfamiliar song and want to know the name and artist, ask your phone, "What is this song?" Then take a screenshot of the answer. You may then look up the complete lyrics of the song to reveal more of the message. Many times, songs that I do not know come to my awareness, and I look them up. Most of the time, the lyrics in my mind indicate the essential parts of the message. Once you determine the message of a song, it can become universally applicable in your life.

Give attention to the songs that resonate with you. Notice what it is about the music that resonates with you. Think about the music you listen to. What are your favorite songs? What are the themes within the lyrics? What rhythm inspires you? Find a song that inspires you. What does the song make you think of? Write about your aspirations and how they relate to the music. Write an inspiring statement. I am frequently inspired by lyrics and write them as messages when they enter my mind. I connect them to what is happening in my life.

The song "Meant to Live" by Switchfoot[5] inspired me to make positive changes in my life. "Whatever it Takes" by Imagine Dragons[6] represents my ongoing persistence. "Freedom" by Pitbull[7] serves as a theme song. What is your theme song? What do you want your theme song to be? Write the theme song that represents what you want to accomplish.

I was listening to "Flashdance…What a Feeling" by Irene Cara[8] while on the way to the Florida Creativity Conference. At the conference, I spent time with an

---

[5] Switchfoot. (2003). "Meant to Live." *The Beautiful Letdown*. Columbia Records.

[6] Imagine Dragons. (2017). "Whatever it Takes." *Evolve*. Interscope Records.

[7] Pitbull. (2016). "Freedom." *Climate Change*. RCA Records.

[8] Irene Cara. (1983). "Flashdance…What a Feeling." *What a Feelin'*. Geffen Records.

absolute legend in the creativity field. She was so warm and wanted to share her extraordinary wisdom with me. I felt enchanted and ready to forge ahead after our time together. I have kept "Flashdance…What a Feeling" present in my mind as a reminder of this beautiful experience and inspiration to keep going. Whenever the song comes to mind, I know it will be a good day.

What is the soundtrack of your life? Create a timeline of the soundtrack of your life so far. How do you feel about your soundtrack? If you love it, keep it. If not, ask yourself, is this who you want to be? Who is the person within? Be who you are. Believe in yourself. Let your voice be heard. Courageously go after what you want. Follow your intuition and allow the music to inspire you to become the person you were meant to be.

Creating a soundtrack can be a fun and collaborative experience. We spent days building a soundtrack at the simulation center. While setting up for a medication distribution lab, we would play "Purple Pills" by D12[9] and "Another One Bites the Dust" by Queen[10] when a mannequin would not operate.

---

[9] D12. (2001). "Purple Pills." *Devil's Night*. Shady Records. Interscope Records.
[10] Queen. (1980). "Another One Bites the Dust." *The Game*. Elektra Records.

"Somebody's Watching Me" by Rockwell[11] applied to how simulations were remotely viewed on surveillance. My favorites were "Crazy" by Gnarls Barkley[12] and "Barbie Girl" by Aqua[13], as I was wearing a mannequin's face, arms, and right foot for Halloween.

The songs we played created a hilarious and fun workday for all of us. All our lyrical intuition grew as we spoke to one another in lyrics.

Notice songs as they randomly pop into your head. Wonder what they mean and make the connection. Which type of music activates your intuition? Sometimes when a liar speaks, I hear "Little Lies" by Fleetwood Mac[14] drowning out whatever they say. I know the truth is not surfacing if that song enters my mind.

Often songs pop into my head randomly, or I will hear a song and find meaning within the lyrics. The songs are not always spontaneous. I have been able to scan my mind and find an available song. You can provoke the songs available in your mind without

---

[11] Rockwell & Michael Jackson (1984). "Somebody's Watching Me." *Somebody's Watching Me*. Motown Records.
[12] Gnarls Barkley. (2006). "Crazy." *St. Elsewhere*. Atlantic Records.
[13] Aqua. (1997). "Barbie Girl." *Aquarium*. Universal Music Group.
[14] Fleetwood Mac. (1987). "Little Lies." *Tango in the Night*. Warner Brothers.

turning on the music in the following activity. This will help you activate your musical intuition.

Provocation of Musical Intuition Action Steps:

- Scan your mind until you notice any song that comes into your awareness.
- Write the lyrics as they come to mind.
- Notice what else is on your mind.
- Write your thoughts as you listen to the song.
- How do your thoughts relate to the lyrics?
- What is the connection between the song and the other things on your mind?
- Write the message of the song as it relates to your life.

Music provides an intuitive foreshadowing of upcoming events. When you wake up to the day, notice if there is music playing in your mind. Write the lyrics and be mindful as the day progresses to determine the meaning. One morning I woke up with "We're Good" by Dua Lipa[15] in my head. At a mid-morning Zoom meeting, a consultant asked me to provide him with my intellectual property for his consulting business. There would be no payment or recognition for my contribution. At that moment, I knew the song had

---

[15] Dua Lipa. (2021). "We're Good." *Future Nostalgia: The Moonlight Edition*. Warner Records.

significance for this meeting. I politely declined and continued along on my own path.

Sometimes a song will lead to another sign or a series of signs. Each sign contributes to the intuitive application of the song lyrics to your life. I am more alert to my surroundings when I pay attention to the lyrics. The lyrics serve as a guide. At times they serve as a notification for me to make better decisions. I woke up with "Astronaut in the Ocean" by Masked Wolf[16] playing in my mind. Then I saw the image of an astronaut and scuba diver on Pinterest. Next, I saw a picture of an astronaut in an email for a conference.

I asked, "What is the message?"

I wrote: "Be in my bubble, protected from outside forces. Explore in a self-contained solo bubble as a new world expands around me."

When someone asked me to co-present a workshop at the conference, I knew the application of the astronaut messages. I felt that song. Like my incredible solo dive experience in Chapter 1, I could follow along, but it would cramp my style. I will have a much better experience if I go solo and do my own thing.

---

[16] Masked Wolf. (2019). "Astronaut in the Ocean." *Astronaut in the Ocean.* Elektra Records.

"Rhythm is a Dancer" by Snap![17] was prevalent in my mind as I was leaving Florida, months before I would return and discover the song's relevance. I had an excellent collaborative training session with a creativity champion at the Florida Creativity Conference. The song popped into my head as I co-presented the Foundations of Creative Problem Solving course. We were talking about songs that speak to the moments and times of our lives. Just like that, "Rhythm is a Dancer" by Snap! had meaning as this song represented how I felt about our excellent co-facilitator dynamic and our lovely group of participants in the session. The song was right on. I knew that I would return to Sarasota, and I knew that it would be great. I only knew the details once I was in the situation.

When a song is stuck in your head, there might be something in your life that the song is calling to your attention. Write out the lyrics and pay attention. Be patient and allow the music to show you the meaning. Pay attention, and you will make the connection. Once you determine the application, the song will typically stop. If it continues, you still need to figure out the proper application. The meaning could also be about an ongoing theme in your life. It may be about a more significant issue. One summer, "Dust in the Wind" by

---

[17] Snap! (1992). "Rhythm is a Dancer." *The Madman's Return.* Arista, Logic.

Kansas[18] was stuck in my head. My dog Riley died that summer. The song stopped. Six weeks later, the song popped into my mind as I approached a friend. She told me that her dog had just died. Chills went down my spine.

Music plays at the precise moment. "I Won't Back Down" by Tom Petty[19] was playing on the car stereo. I raised the volume and told my son to listen to the song as my advice to him. Earlier that day, he had told me his plan to stop school bullies from targeting him. The music conveyed what I was unable to articulate. The song arrived at the perfect moment in time. Songs appear as affirmative support to say what we want to express in a way that gives a compelling message.

For many years, I have wanted to write a book to share my way of navigating the world in the hopes that my stories would inspire others to explore, have fun, and trust their way of navigating the world. In a moment of uncertainty, I considered writing a more academic text about research and other books. "Would anyone care to read about my intuitive journey through life?" Suddenly, I felt a cold breeze on my lips and heard the song "Unwritten" by Natasha Bedingfield[20]. The song arrived

---

[18] Kansas. (1977). "Dust in the Wind." *Point of Know Return.* Kirshner.

[19] Tom Petty. (1989). "I Won't Back Down." *Full Moon Fever.* MCA Records, Inc.

[20] Natasha Bedingfield. (2004). "Unwritten." *Unwritten.* BMG UK & Ireland. Epic Records.

as confirmation. I felt a sense of calm assurance, knowing I would share my personal, quirky stories.

"Good Vibrations" by Marky Mark and the Funky Bunch[21] popped into my head when I saw a 1990s picture of Mark Wahlberg in my news feed. Then as I was driving, I clicked the buttons on the stored radio stations in the car, and "Good Vibrations" was playing loud and clear on a station that is usually inaudible static. It has been about thirty years since that image and song were broadcast frequently.

Signs appear through genres of music from my youth. The signs will appear in the things you appreciate or associate with. From these references, notice what happens next as the message may appear in the next thing you encounter. The next song was about gratitude and sharing resources with others to bring them joy. This was yet another confirmation to continue writing this book.

Activate your musical intuition in the following activity.

Follow the Lyrics Action Steps:

- Listen to a song.
- Focus on the lyrics.
- What does the song mean to you?

---

[21] Marky Mark and the Funky Bunch. (1991). "Good Vibrations." *Music for the People.* Interscope Records.

- What connections do you make to the lyrics?
- Notice repeated themes within the song that speak to aspects of your life.
- How does the song parallel your life?
- Write about what you discover.

Encourage your musical intuition by listening for a daily message in the lyrics of a song. Be cognizant of any music you hear or songs that enter your mind. Notice the words and write the lyrics that are most present in your mind. Reflect on what the words mean to you. Take note of what is going on in your life as well. Make the connection between the song and your life.

In the same way that homing pigeons use infrasound to navigate their way, we can become attuned to sound in the form of music to navigate our way. When you first wake up, scan your mind to reveal any songs foreshadowing the day or articulating what will happen in the future. Be authentic and feel the music within. Let it out—the lyrics, the dance, and the rhythmic symphony of life. If there are songs that speak to your wishes, keep them present to assist your intuitive discovery on the path to actualizing your wishes. Musical intuition will become stronger with practice.

Chapter 10:

Intuitive Writing

When my time as a graduate student ended, I wrote from my intuition to figure out what I aspired to do. I wrote the following:

"I want to write a book with depth and intensity of emotion about what hasn't been expressed to explore emotionality and the unknown uninhibited realms of self. Focus on the values of the individual and the strength they bring from multiple perspectives. Everyone has a unique story constructed from the same event."

I wrote questions and answers. "What would I be most happy doing? I like applying creativity techniques to encourage others to think of possibilities. I want to work remotely from wherever I want. Teach a creativity course from a distance. Photograph my experiences and inspire others to do the same. People attend my workshops to experience Wild in Sight. These workshops could be at places I travel to, virtually, or in person near where I live. I want to develop a business consisting of books, keynote speeches, workshops I present worldwide, and online courses. What qualities do I bring? I bring intellect, creativity, persistence, adventure, loyalty, and love. The qualities I have that I will share are authenticity, openness, and support. I will help others develop calm introspection. What keywords define what I want to do? Creativity, inspiration, growth, passion, nature, discovering, exploring, adventure, writing, and photography."

The results of this intuitive writing were as follows: Two years after this writing, a global pandemic occurred, and my work became remote. The Wild in Sight photography workshops were successful at virtual and live conferences among a worldwide audience. I became part of the core faculty for the Creative Education Foundation, teaching creativity courses from a distance and at both of the Creative Education Foundation's in-person conferences: Creative Problem Solving Institute and Florida Creativity Conference. This book you are reading is exactly what I wanted to write. Much of this book was generated through intuitive writing.

Writing offers insights beyond conscious thought into another realm of possibility. Writing may create an experience of transcendence beyond the normal. Write what you want to develop and bring into your life.

Create your own story with depth and precision. Whatever comes to mind, write it down without editing or worrying about spelling or punctuation. Let the writing free flow in any way, and write anything that comes to mind. This free-flowing technique is sometimes poetic and sometimes prophetic. Just keep writing. The more you write, the more likely you are to receive a unique intuitive message. As you write, the message will become more revealing.

Writing is an introspective activity that allows you to tap into a deeper level of consciousness. As you write, you enter a trance-like state of flow and write from within, exposing the depth of your awareness to yourself.

Intuitive Writing Action Steps:

- Write about what is on your mind.
- Write everything that comes to mind.
- Ask a question that answers.
- Ask another question to discover more.
- If you write something that fascinates you, elaborate on it.
- Play with the sequence of the words that you write.

Practice the free-flowing technique to discover what is within your mind and ready to be revealed. Sometimes the writing may remain poetic and seemingly irrelevant. Save the beautiful writing; one day, the message will appear clearly when you read it. Select any other activity in this book to write about, such as observing a photo or reflecting on a song. Apply intuitive writing to discover answers, determine the meaning of a song, interpret a photograph, or during nature admiration.

Create a metaphor or analogy. When we think metaphorically or analogically, we take ideas or words from one context and apply them to another context to generate new idea combinations. When we see things in the context of their relationships with other things, it helps to expand our perception.

I create a few metaphors to read later on. As time goes by, the analogies remind me that I am on the right path. The analogy I made about my visit to the Allan Gardens Conservatory laid the foundation for my workshops and this book.

The analogy: "This is my garden of life that I am meant to cultivate and grow and bloom from within and share wild wisdom with the world like seeds of inspiration to spark growth and inspire action for others to blossom."

A woman in one of my workshops took pictures of reflections. She focused on the word, physical appearance, and the concept of reflection. She shared her introspective experience on reflection with a series of metaphoric statements as follows: "Perfection in Reflection," "Reflect Perfection," "Create a Reflection to Become the Image of Perfection," and "Create an Image of Perfection to Become a Reflection." Upon completion, she shared that she did not want to hide in the background as a reflection. She planned to share her perspective more actively.

Use a word or concept to generate metaphors, and then notice where else the word shows up to determine the message. Do you ever notice a word or concept that suddenly appears to be everywhere? Beginning with a dream, one day, the word "edge" was everywhere: in movies, songs, news, and emails. I collected them in writing. As the day went on, intuition provided the message. "There is ambiguity at the edge, and with a push, you know it's time to fly and soar to new heights. It's time to stop standing at the edge of life and take the leap. There will be new beginnings and celebrations in flight."

Aspire to create an inspirational metaphor that propels you forward. Customize a metaphor that inspires you in the action steps below.

Create a Metaphor Action Steps:

- Reflect on a word, image, or collection of words and images.
- Write statements comparing the word or image to something else.
- Compare this statement to an aspect of your life.
- Generate statements in comparison.

- Play with the order and sequence of the words in the statements.

When we take the time to create metaphors, we can extract our inner intuitive thoughts that are hidden from our daily conscious awareness. This process provides another way to expand beyond patterned thinking that disregards unfamiliar ideas. Metaphors may expose universally applicable timeless guidance to many aspects of our lives. The abstract presentation of metaphors and poetic writing helps you get in touch with your unknown inner brilliance. You reveal what is hidden within and ready to be expressed as you write.

Sometimes the precise meaning of an abstract concept remains out of focus until you enter the moment in which it was meant to be applied. When the moment occurs, it is an aha moment—an internal moment of *Yes, this is what that meant.* Sometimes you will experience a feeling of recollection that you knew what would happen, and it happened, yet you remain uncertain of how you knew. Review what you have written occasionally to determine the patterns in which your intuitive brilliance speaks to you. What you discover may encourage you to write more to reveal what you already knew precognitively.

Chapter 11:

Dreams

Occasionally, intuitive messages will arrive in the form of dreams or nightmares. When you wake up, write down what you recall about your dreams in order to become conscious of the messages. Sometimes the dream will give you a quick flash of intuition that may vanish as quickly as it arrived. If you ever wake up with a message, write it immediately before falling asleep or forgetting it. Document the message at the moment before it fades away. Write it down, even when it seems simple and well-known to you. It is also helpful to practice intuitive writing after waking from a dream to reveal the entirety of a message while already in a relaxed state of enhanced receptivity.

You may experience words that you never use coming to your awareness in dreams. Write the words as they come. Especially notice when they are words that you do not typically use. Trust that they mean something.   Initially, you may not know the exact application for the message. Unusual words may appear in dreams and other formats that tie together and reveal the   application   of   the   message.   The   word "conflagration" was spoken to me in a dream and then appeared in a description of the lover's tarot card. What does that word mean?   "It means flame, rekindle, and passion. Love is a choice. My passion and love are my power." The conflagration was a reminder to keep doing what I love.

The words that arrive in dreams are sometimes words I would not speak or typically hear. I dreamt I was on a plane and an older couple wanted to see my boarding pass until I went to show it to them and chased after them in the airport, still trying to show it to them. Then a young red-headed man told me he used to be like me chasing people away, even the ones he cared about. I asked how to stop.

He said, "Stop trying to prove yourself to people who don't matter and give your attention to those who care. Don't wield away power in the chase. Wielding takes power away."

I never use the word wield, which was proof of intuition speaking.

Another way to receive dream guidance is to ask for it. Ask what you want to know or ask a question using questions that answer. Before going to sleep, I welcomed guidance and dreams and asked, "What are my next steps?"

That night I dreamt of being on stage wearing a purple and gold dress. I felt excited and comfortable in the environment. The next day, I was at T.J. Maxx, and there it was; the purple and gold dress just like the one I was wearing on stage in that dream. I tried it on and could feel the energy of my Grandma Olga in the purple and my son in the fish stitched in gold metallic thread. My mother had previously given me a gift card that would cover the exact cost. I bought the dress. As of this writing, the stage appearance has yet to arrive. Perhaps it is coming at a time beyond my current knowledge or level of awareness.

Dreams are a way for your intuition to come through without your resistance. Notice if anything that you dream appears while you are awake. Follow the action steps below to activate your dream intuition.

Dream Intuition Action Steps:

- Indicate that you welcome dream intuition.
- Ask, "What are my next steps?"
- As soon as you wake up, document the dream and message.
- Reflect on the meaning.
  - o How does the dream connect with anything that is happening currently?

- o What is upcoming that the dream may be providing information about?
- o What are the similarities between your dream and your life?
- o Apply intuitive writing to discover the meaning.
- o Consult tarot or oracle cards to reveal the meaning.
- o Pay attention during the day and see if there are additional connections.

Dreams are my strongest point of access to precognitive knowledge. Many applicable metaphors and comparative sequences of events from my dreams will happen in my life. I have learned over the years to believe in my dreams and nightmares. Dreams show me glimpses of positive times ahead. Sometimes the dreams provide repetitions revealing people that I will meet, places I will go, and success that will come. Nightmares warn me of bad outcomes and protect me from destructive relationships and situations. Sometimes nightmares show me exaggerated worst-case scenarios that I cannot overlook. When I receive this presentation, I know to be vigilant.

Imagine you awaken in the middle of a nightmare. There is nothing you can do because your body is unable to move. Sleep paralysis occurs when you wake up still in a dream state. The condition has appeared sporadically since I was a teenager. When it happens to me, my mind is cognizant that I am in a dream and can mentally act against the terror. My body is immobilized, and I am unable to speak out loud. While mentally awake and unable to move, I have had many nightmares in which I felt like many hands or some entity was holding me down. I always try to keep my mind disengaged from the terror of the nightmare.

After a night of sleep paralysis, I woke in a nightmare where men in suits were insulting me and sucking my breath away as I refused to hear the words spoken and fought to awaken from the dream state as fast as possible. I felt shock waves of an electric current running down my temples, which helped me not hear or entertain the words of criticism. An inspirational song entered my mind as I waited for the state of sleep paralysis to end.

I use the occurrences of sleep paralysis to learn as I fight to fully wake out of the terror and resist the nightmare. In the sleep paralysis nightmare above, I realized I am strong, confident, and worthy. "I know that I have the skills to save myself. The words of these toxic figures do not matter. I will not hear them. I know the way, and I get out safely. Fancy suits and mean words do not define me and will not overpower me. I will do what is best, safest, and most life-sustaining. I will leave toxic people and situations behind. This is my life. I will protect it and spend it doing what is best for me. I will not listen to my value in the opinion of others. Close the door and walk away. Vibe out, level up, and prosper."

By reframing and resisting the nightmare, I have reduced the frequency of sleep paralysis occurrences.

My son also experiences sleep paralysis. I told him that I was writing about sleep paralysis in this book. His perspective differs from mine. He finds humor in the absurdity and thinks sleep paralysis is funny because it rarely happens. Then we discussed how the event is better than a horror movie because it is an entirely immersive experience. Our perspective on events impacts our understanding of them. Changing our perspective on an event clears any stagnant energy that blocks the way forward.

I use the approach below when I am feeling fear amid sleep paralysis. It is an effective way to overcome fear or heightened emotions in other circumstances too. I have taught teenagers how to use this method to disengage from a verbal attack. A mind that is focused on cognition will disconnect from an emotional state. The math sequence provides a neutral cognitive task to focus on while entering a calm, relaxed state. Selecting a song will assist in generating positive emotions. This technique will calm the mind, body, and emotions.

Overcome Sleep Paralysis or Fears Action Steps:

- Focus on a math sequence such as 1 times 1 is 1, 2 times 2 is 4, etc., until you are disengaged from the heightened emotional state.
- Focus on a song that inspires you and play the words in your mind.
- What strengths are you applying as you resist the situation?
- What are you learning from the occurrence?

Nightmares are just a dark negative counterpart to a positive dream sequence. Dreams and nightmares both include intuitive advice that you can use to improve the quality of your life. Reframe the nightmares and heed the warning to minimize the frequency of recurrent nightmares. Just like any other form of intuition, if you ignore the message, it may haunt you.

Consider sleep as an opportunity for intuition to arrive at night. Ask about what you want guidance on before going to sleep. Trust that you will wake up with a message. Welcome unexpected sequences to show you what's on the horizon.

Chapter 12:

Live Your Wild

Wild intuition thrives in a state of creative awareness. Strive to notice the things that spark a warm feeling of excitement and awe. An internal knowing of *Yes, this is it. This is what I am looking for. This is what I am here for.* Be vibrant. Recognize your intuitive strengths. You will synthesize knowledge into action. Love and live according to the divine essence. Celebrate harmoniously as you discover your wild. Live your truth and share it. Live life to the fullest. Experience all that life offers. What do you bring on this adventure? Write and observe to reveal the message.

Imagine the tightly compressed bud of a flower. The flower must connect with all its surroundings to bloom. The flower is influenced and developed by environmental conditions such as temperature, sun, rain, and the activities of other organisms such as insects, animals, and plants. The flower must bloom at the appropriate time to ensure the survival and production of seeds to share with the ecosystem. Just as a flower must bloom, we must let the wild out to spread joy, love, and inspiration. Begin to open and bloom like flowers in the sun—awake, aware, and alive. Awaken your wild intuition with an open heart, sharp intuition, and connected spirit.

Allow natural growth. Each of us grows and evolves in our own way. Let it be as it is, and let it grow in its own time. Growth and lasting stability are free of force and enter their way of enlightenment. The sun radiates. The wind connects. The rain cleanses. Allow spacious adoration in an open sky. Radiant sun. Transformative light and warmth. Growing and accumulating worldly knowledge strengthens the union and transition of form. Become the flower you were meant to be in the golden light.

Determine what you most want from your life. What is the very best that you could do? Search for your highest potential. Set good aspirations. Fantasy precedes reality so visualize the reality you want to create. Gain a visual in your mind of your best aspirations. Feel the sensations and emotions as if you are living those aspirations now. Write the narrative of the adventure you desire. Apply intuitive writing to add the details that will bring the story to life. Take photos as reminders and for encouragement. Seek the guidance of your intuition as you develop the plan. Take the steps as they appear.

Step in and live that reality today. Find the songs that inspire and add excitement to the story. Ask your dreams to show you the way. Look for inspiration and confirmation in the world around you. Be genuine and authentic. Life is limitless. Perceive the world in a new way among the geographic elements of natural connection. Display and share, collaborate, and co-create the exquisite experience. Expansive thinking leads the journey to abundant intuition. You are the genius of your life.

Access your intuitive gifts. Accept who you truly are. Have the confidence to illuminate your wild. Attractive opportunities to actualize desires and wishes will occur. You are making it all happen now. Keep going. Reflective magnetic light rays expand and echo, bringing in abundant opportunities. Be courageous, energetic, free-spirited, determined, and successful. Continue on the adventure of creative awareness with lots of energy and enthusiasm. Be willing to listen to your soul's guidance and choose love with love.

Imagine being surrounded by white light with unconditional radiant healing love. Feel the love emanating vibrationally. Love intensifies. Join in unity on a journey of higher vision. The bonds exist infinitely within eternity, even for only a moment—past, present, and future—unbound by time in which destiny and all majesty recur and vibrate spiritually. The union shall occur at the precise destined moment of which we are unaware. Tremendous love from all dimensions awaits. Love is timeless, and it comes in its own time.

Follow your intuition to stay on the path of love. Focus on love and truth. Genuine connection inspires you to love more deeply and fearlessly. The world is perceived differently at different levels of consciousness. More connection and exploration allow access to the elemental heights. The radiant feeling increases when you are more profoundly connected and trance-like. Now is the time. Dance to the rhythm of your soul and dance with the rhythm of life. Be authentic, as anything less than genuine authenticity is harmful. Be who you truly are.

What is your wild? How do you nurture it? Where does your wild show up in your life? How do you connect your wild with the wisdom within? To be wild is to be free. Let the wild out! Experience the beauty of your wild as you increase your wild intuition.

The intuitive is universally applicable. Intuition comes from within. The world shapes you as it gives you intuitive messages. Believe in your dreams and trust your intuition. Intensely pursue what fascinates you and follow the guideposts of your intuition to make it a reality. Close the gap between dreams and reality by acting daily to reveal the connection. Live the truth of your intuition. Allow the expression of the message. Wild intuition is only limited by the potential to receive. Trust the timing that shows when to proceed. If you keep taking the best action steps as they appear, the steps will continue to appear along the journey. Go with what feels most right at any given moment. Channel your inner map into an ocean of magnificence and transcendental growth, expanding to reach the beautiful island of paradise and overall elation in the universe. Treasure and enjoy the journey. Love, honor, and welcome your inner sense of knowing to guide the way.

To be wild is to be authentic. Authenticity is a navigator that clearly defines the most optimal direction for you to go. Permit yourself to receive the guidance to get there. Acceptance of your authenticity opens the space to bring about the truest potential in your life. If you design a space where dreams are welcome, they will occur. Generate a mindset of readiness to create the future. Remain clear and focused while navigating the path. Have the willingness to receive intuitive guidance. Make requests of your intuition. Believe in the information you receive. Once known, take decisive action. Say "Yes" to new opportunities. There is potential everywhere. Intuition represents authentic truth. Be flexible and dare to live a life defined by wild intuition.

The future is composed of our present everyday moments. Fulfill your potential in the best way. Keep moving forward on the journey with the wisdom of your wild intuition.

In time a continuous adventure in creative awareness may become your way of life. Follow the path of loving guidance from your wild intuition. Live your wild.

References in Order of Appearance

Simple Plan. (2002). "The Worst Day Ever" [Song]. *No Pads, No Helmets...Just Balls* [Album]. Lava Records. Atlantic Records.

Beastie Boys. (1994). "Sabotage" [Song]. *Ill Communication* [Album]. Grand Royal Records. Capitol Records.

OK Go. (2010). "This Too Shall Pass" [Song]. *Of the Blue Colour of the Sky* [Album]. Capitol Records.

The Doors. (1971). Riders of the storm [Song]. On *L.A. woman* [Album]. Elektra Records.

Switchfoot. (2003). Meant to live [Song]. *The beautiful letdown* [Album]. Columbia Records.

Imagine Dragons. (2017). Whatever it takes [Song]. *Evolve* [Album]. Interscope Records.

Pitbull. (2016). Freedom [Song]. *Climate change* [Album]. RCA Records.

Irene Cara. (1983). Flashdance...what a feeling [Song]. *What a feelin'* [Album]. Geffen Records.

D12. (2001). Purple pills [Song]. *Devil's night* [Album]. Shady Records. Interscope Records.

Queen. (1980). Another one bites the dust [Song]. *The game* [Album]. Elektra Records.

Rockwell & Michael Jackson (1984). Somebody's watching me [Song]. *Somebody's watching me* [Album]. Motown Records.

Gnarls Barkley. (2006). Crazy [Song]. *St. Elsewhere* [Album]. Atlantic Records.

Aqua. (1997). Barbie girl [Song]. *Aquarium* [Album]. Universal Music Group.

Fleetwood Mac. (1987). Little lies [Song]. *Tango in the night* [Album]. Warner Brothers.

Dua Lipa. (2021). We're good [Song]. On *Future nostalgia: the moonlight edition* [Album]. Warner Brothers.

Masked Wolf. (2019). Astronaut in the ocean [Song]. *Astronaut in the ocean* [Album]. Elektra Records.

Snap! (1992). Rhythm is a dancer [Song]. *The madman's return* [Album]. Arista Logic.

Kansas. (1977). Dust in the wind [Song]. *Point of know return* [Album]. Kirshner.

Tom Petty. (1989). I won't back down [Song]. *Full moon fever* [Album]. MCA.

Natasha Bedingfield. (2004). Unwritten [Song]. *Unwritten* [Album]. BMG UK & Ireland. Epic Records.

Marky Mark and the Funky Bunch. (1991). Good vibrations [Song]. *Music for the people* [Album]. Interscope Records.

About the Author

Melissa Wild has a Master's Degree in Creativity and Change Leadership from the Center for Applied Imagination at Buffalo State University. She completed Erickson Professional Coach Certification in Canada and PADI Advanced Open Water Diver Certification in Mexico. Melissa is an international conference presenter.